DEDICATION

I dedicate this book to my wonderful Dog who is already in Dog Heaven - Luna. I love and miss You very much. I hope that You are happy up there, You have your soft cloud from which You look down and we will meet again sometime. See You...

Do you believe there is a Heaven for Dogs? Somewhere high above the clouds... A wonderful place in the World, where they run in the meadows, jump on the clouds, have fun, and always have a full bowl? I'll tell you a wonderful story about a mutt whose name was Lucky...

I would like to introduce Lucky and this is his most beloved lady in the world – 7 years old Nel. When he first met her, he immediately fell in love with his doggy heart. Nel takes care of him, feeds him, takes him out for walks, plays with him and they even sleep together.

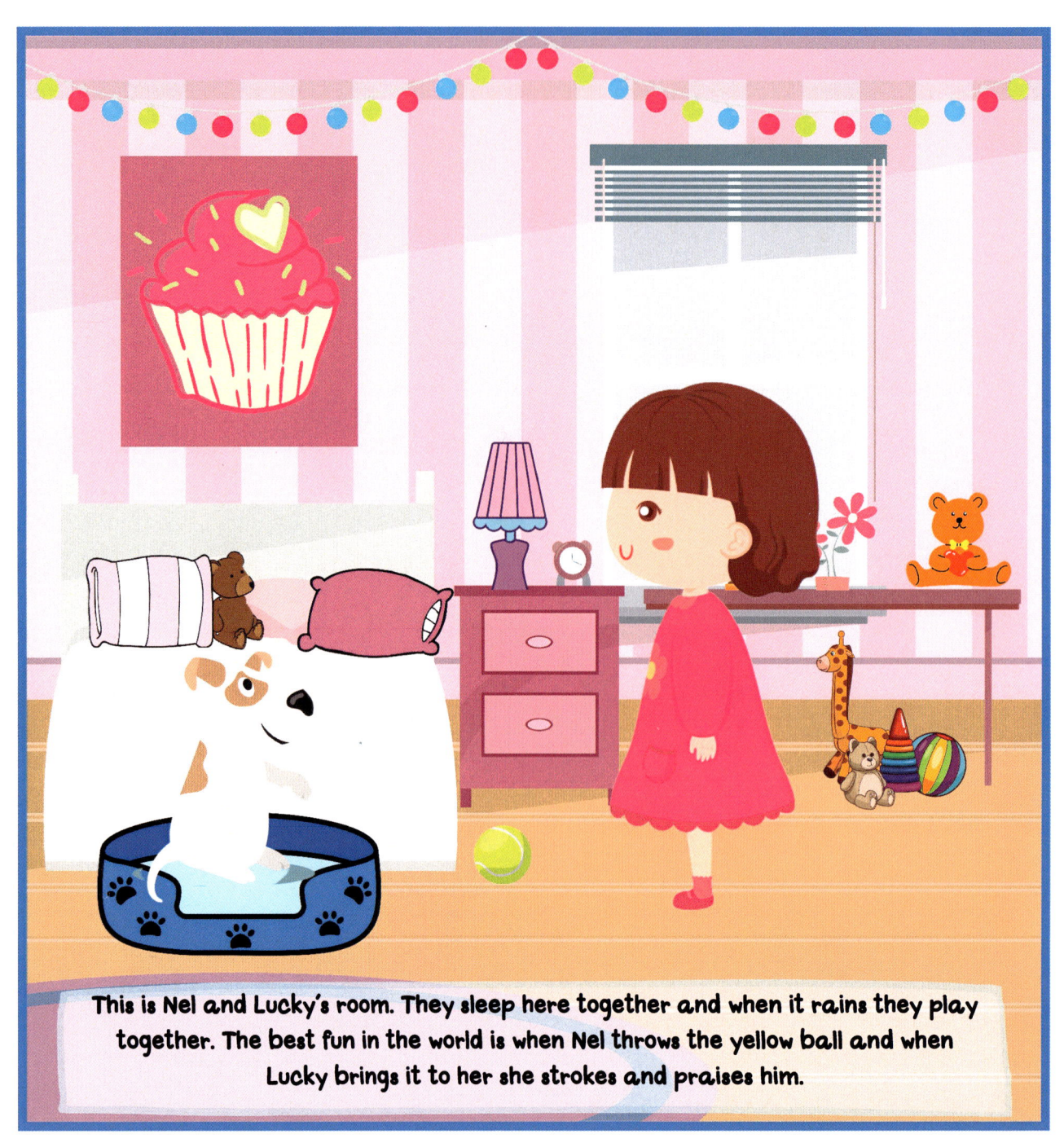

This is Nel and Lucky's room. They sleep here together and when it rains they play together. The best fun in the world is when Nel throws the yellow ball and when Lucky brings it to her she strokes and praises him.

Lucky even accompanies Nel in the bath. Together they fool around in a bathtub full of foam. Lucky tries to catch all the soap bubbles.

A walk in the park together makes for a perfect afternoon. Lucky runs by Nela, chasing the butterflies that are flying by. He loves to fetch a thrown stick or fetch his favorite yellow ball.

While Nel is playing with her friends on the playground, Lucky always takes a break for a short nap in the shade of the trees.

Winter

Summer

Spring

Autumn

Days have passed...

One day, when Nel came home from school, Mom announced that they needed to have a very serious talk. Nel felt that something was wrong because Mom looked very sad.

Mom calmly explained to Nel that Lucky had gone. The dog had a very sick heart... He fell asleep and went to heaven...

Nel was very touched by the loss of her best friend... She never forgot him and always had him in her heart...

Lucky opened one eye, then the other. There was darkness. After a moment, he noticed a bright light shining somewhere in the distance. He thought that maybe if he followed it, he would get home.

The light began to get brighter and bigger with each step. "What could it be?" - thought Lucky.

Suddenly there was a huge staircase, which was very soft as he climbed it. At the very top there was something, but he could not see what, because it was so far away.

In the middle of the road, a sign appeared that read "Dogs Heaven." Lucky thought maybe it was some kind of dog park. He always went there with Nel and played with his dog friends. He decided to go see what it was, and then he wanted to look for a way home....

Climbing all those stairs was so tiring that Lucky decided to take a short nap.

Suddenly, Lucky woke up as the big gate began to open. Curious, he got up quickly and began to enter the Dog Paradise. "Strange these clouds" - he thought as he saw a dog-shaped cloud flying past him.

Suddenly a huge and twisting rainbow slide appeared outside the gate. Lucky wanted to back out but he had no way anymore. He started to slide down and down and down...

Suddenly there was a beautiful meadow full of fragrant flowers and lots of different dogs running around. They were all happy and smiling and... they had wings. "Where am I?" - thought Lucky with astonishment.

Lucky looked around slowly. Everywhere was beautiful, with lots of colorful flowers, bushes, and trees. Suddenly an unknown doggie came up to him "Hi I'm Luna, welcome to doggy heaven, I'll explain everything to you, don't be sad"

Luna told about this "strange" place: "This is a dog's paradise. Dogs that have left the earth live here. There is no disease, misery, or sadness here. All of us here have a carefree life and are happy. We have wings to fly, to slide down the rainbow and to jump on the clouds".

They flew on. Suddenly it became quiet, and all around them, they could hear a gentle gust of wind and a sort of quiet very relaxing melody. "Those are clouds of rest." - Luna said. This is where all the Doggies come to nap, they jump on one of the clouds and its down wraps them up to sleep.

They arrived at a place that smelled of food. They were salivating from the smell of meat. "This is where we eat". - Luna announced - "You will find everything you like here, meat, dog food, dog treats, bones, and water. The food here never ends."

Time passed. Lucky and Luna became very good friends. They ran around with each other all day and played more and more games. Lucky was very happy and had a lot of fun, but...

Although he had many new friends, his tummy was always full and he was healthy and happy, he still felt that he had an emptiness in his heart. He missed his Nel very much.

The years passed... many years...One day while playing with Luna, Lucky smelled something... a familiar smell. He
stopped in shock, started running as fast as he could, tears coming to his eyes....
He had to check something...

He knew the way exactly, he could smell it more and more, his nose was not wrong.
He knew exactly who was standing there...

It WAS NEL!!! The joy was endless! They both cried for a long time and hugged each other tightly. Lucky was the happiest dog in the world and in all of heaven.

Love Forever

Nel sprouted wings after crossing the gate. They didn't need anything to be happy anymore. Those two stayed there TOGETHER FOREVER....

THE END

There is only one downside to having a dog – farewell...

ONE LAST THING...

If you enjoyed this book or found it useful I'd be vary grateful if you'd post a short review on Amazon. Your support really does make a difference and I read all the reviews personally so I can get Your feedback and make this book even better!
Thanks again for your support :)

Illustrations used from : Vecteezy, Freeplik

Manufactured by Amazon.ca
Bolton, ON